UNITED STATES AND AFRICA: INTO THE TWENTY-FIRST CENTURY

POLICY ESSAY NO. 7

UNITED STATES AND AFRICA:

INTO THE TWENTY-FIRST CENTURY

CAROL J. LANCASTER

OVERSEAS DEVELOPMENT COUNCIL
WASHINGTON, DC

Library of Congress Cataloging-in-Publication Data

Lancaster, Carol J.
  United States and Africa: into the twenty-first century/Carol J. Lancaster

Policy Essay No. 7
Includes bibliographical references.
    1. Africa—Foreign relations—United States. 2. United States—Foreign relations—Africa. 3. United States—Foreign relations—1945–1989. 4. United States—Foreign relations—1989–   I. Title. II. Series.

DT38.L36   1993   327.7306—dc20   93-19138 CIP

ISBN: 1-56517-010-5

Printed in the United States of America.

Director of Publications: Christine E. Contee
Publications Editor: Jacqueline Edlund-Braun
Edited by Kathleen A. Lynch
Cover and book design by Tim Kenney Design Partners, Inc.
Map by Design Consultants of Virginia, Inc.

Contents

Foreword vii

Executive Summary 1

Part I. Introduction 5

Part II. Sub-Saharan Africa Today 9

   Political Patterns of Development, 1960–1990 10

   Economic Trends Since the 1960s 14

   First Steps Toward Political Liberalization 16

   Marginalization of Africa 18

Part III. Three Key African Challenges 21

   Civil Conflict 22

      Causes of Conflict Beyond the Cold War 22

      The Cold War Legacy 25

   Democratization 26

      The Shape of Democracy in Africa 27

   Development 34

      Impact of Economic Policy Reform 35

      Economies of the CFA 37

      Roadblocks to Reform 39

Part IV. United States and Africa: Into the Twenty-First Century . . . 45

   Resolving Civil Conflicts 46

A New U.S. Conflict Resolution Policy 47

Supporting Democracy in Africa 49

U.S. Policy to Promote African Democracy 50

Supporting Development 53

Putting It All Together 56

Notes 58

Acknowledgments 60

About the Author 60

About the ODC 61

Board of Directors 62

Foreword

In its first months, the Clinton administration has had to deal with crises in Africa, chiefly the military relief effort in Somalia, but also the increasingly unstable situation in Zaïre and the deterioration in Sudan and Angola, among other potential trouble spots. In this *Policy Essay*, Carol Lancaster analyzes three of the critical challenges now facing Africa—resolving civil conflict, supporting nascent efforts at political pluralism, and promoting sustainable development—and presents a series of possible U.S. policy responses. Dr. Lancaster is the current ODC Davidson Sommers Fellow.

As U.S. domestic and foreign policy priorities are realigned in the months ahead, the question is likely to be asked, why should the United States care about Africa? As Lancaster observes, our already minimal strategic interests in the continent have greatly diminished and our economic relations remain marginal. But a compelling rationale for a continuing U.S. engagement in Africa remains: U.S. foreign policy has always been in part a reflection of American values, of which promoting free societies and sustainable economic development overseas as well as relieving human suffering are a part. In addition, there is a significant U.S. constituency for Africa that has grown in strength in the 1980s.

The *Policy Essay* series provides a forum for authors to express opinions, make predictions, and assess policy ramifications in the field of U.S.-developing country relations. The relatively abbreviated format is short enough to serve as a digestible brief for policymaking, yet lengthy enough to allow room for more extended analysis.

The Overseas Development Council gratefully acknowledges The Ford Foundation and The Rockefeller Foundation for their support of the Council's overall program; The Hunger Project for support of Dr. Lancaster's research; and the Davidson Sommers Fellowship on International Development Studies for support of Dr. Lancaster's research and publication of this *Policy Essay*. The Davidson Sommers Fellowship, established in 1989, is awarded each year to a distinguished scholar engaged in research and analysis on issues central to the United States and developing countries.

The sweeping changes that have taken place in Africa, the tremendous challenges that remain, and a new U.S. administration combine to require a critical re-examination of U.S. policies toward the region. This essay provides a useful and timely contribution to the forthcoming policy discussion.

John W. Sewell
President
April 1992

Executive Summary

Despite the end of the Cold War and the resulting reduction in U.S. security interests in Sub-Saharan Africa, it still makes sense for the United States to remain diplomatically engaged in the region. Although U.S. economic interests in Africa are small and likely to remain so for the foreseeable future, the values underlying U.S. foreign policy—promoting peace, development, and democracy abroad—argue for active diplomacy. Ten percent of all Americans trace their ancestry to Africa and a growing number of Americans are concerned with events in Africa. This reinforces arguments for U.S. engagement in the region, despite demands on the time and attention of U.S. policymakers that emanate from domestic problems and crises in other parts of the world.

Three major issues confront the United States in its relations with countries of Sub-Saharan Africa now and for the remainder of this century: 1) how to help Africans avoid or resolve civil conflicts, 2) how to assist them to extend and consolidate democracy, and 3) how to support sustainable development in the region.

Civil conflicts have been spreading in Africa over recent years. To help Africans resolve their internal conflicts, the United States should take a two-track approach. In the short run, U.S. action may be needed to mediate conflicts or to intervene directly, as in the case of Somalia. But the United States cannot become the policeman of Africa. It must also persuade or prod the United Nations, the Organization of African Unity, and other appropriate international and regional bodies to develop guidelines for resolving internal conflicts—for example, the circumstances under which external intervention should occur—and to create mechanisms for the resolution of those conflicts, possibly including African or internationally based intervention forces for this purpose. The United States should commit funds to help support peacekeeping forces and appoint a temporary ambassador-at-large to promote international and African action on developing the guidelines and mechanisms needed to deal with these spreading conflicts.

To support the extension and consolidation of democracy in Africa, the new administration should reiterate its commitment to supporting democracy abroad, including in Africa. This commitment should include specific programs such as financial help and training for democratic forces and for newly established democratic governments. Public statements and symbolic acts by the United States in support of democracy can still greatly influence the actions of African leaders and opposition movements. The administration, senior foreign policy officials, and U.S. ambassadors must all act in accord and with a consistent policy in this area. The administration must also ensure to the extent possible that the policies of European governments—above all, that of France whose influence in Francophone Africa remains strong—are coordinated with U.S. policies. Where the United States is alone in advocating democracy, its influence will be greatly diminished. Finally, newly established democracies will ultimately be judged by their peoples on their economic performance—how well they can improve their standard of living. Economic reforms are still urgently needed but must be shaped to avoid destabilizing the new governments. Particularly sensitive policies involve reductions in wages and employment of civil servants, usually organized in unions, which often wield considerable influence with the new regimes.

Development in the region has been very disappointing, despite the large amount of aid thus far provided to African governments. Some of these failures must be attributed to forces beyond the control of Africans, such as adverse trends in the international economy or natural disasters. However, much of the failure is a result of poor policies and weak governance. Economic reforms have not yet led to the increase in private investment that is necessary to drive future growth. The reforms, however, must be maintained and continued if that investment is eventually to come. Meanwhile, it is important that government austerity programs do not result in declines in public investment—especially, in human resource development and the maintenance and expansion of infrastructure—that will be necessary to support healthy future growth. The United States should concentrate its aid in these important areas in the future rather than use its assistance to finance reform programs which, in any case, are developed and negotiated largely by the World Bank and the International Monetary Fund.

In allocating its resources in Sub-Saharan Africa, the United States should most generously aid those governments implementing both political and economic reforms. Those implementing only political *or* economic reforms should receive less assistance. And those governments undertaking no reforms should receive no U.S. aid, except for humanitarian relief.

AFRICA

NOTE: Sub-Saharan African countries indicated in gray.

Part I

Introduction

■   IT IS HIGH TIME THE UNITED STATES assessed its relations with the countries of Sub-Saharan Africa.[1] On taking office, the new U.S. administration has had to deal immediately with crises in Africa after years of drift in U.S. policy toward the region and amid the sweeping changes under way there. Three of the most pressing issues arising from these changes are the focus of this essay: how to address the problems of civil conflict in African societies; how to support democracy in the region; and how to promote sustainable development. Before turning to these issues, however, it is important to address the question so often raised by Americans regarding U.S. policy toward Africa: what interests or values justify a continuing U.S. presence and engagement in Sub-Saharan Africa?

Sub-Saharan Africa has never ranked high among U.S. foreign priorities. The United States has relatively little trade with Africa, currently directing only 1 percent of its exports to the region, and this percentage has been declining over the past decade. U.S. investment in Sub-Saharan Africa is similarly small and, like exports, it is concentrated in two countries—Nigeria and South Africa. It is often argued that African markets could, if more developed, offer the United States important opportunities for trade and investment. This is undoubtedly true; but, given the severe economic problems of the region, it is likely to occur over the long run and does not constitute a persuasive case for an active U.S. engagement in the region today.

With the end of the Cold War, U.S. strategic interests in Africa—never compelling—have greatly diminished. Africa has nearly one-third of the votes in the United Nations General Assembly and three votes in the Security Council—votes that could prove important if the United States wishes to prod the United Nations into a more active role in world affairs or looks to the organization to legitimize U.S. foreign policy. Additionally, the fragility and poverty of African states make them vulnerable to destabilization by outside powers, channels for drug running, and possible venues for terrorist activities—turmoil that can eventually require U.S. policy attention. In other words, the United States does have political interests in Africa, but they are weak.

For continuing an active U.S. engagement in Africa, there are really two rationales. First, U.S. foreign policy is based on more than promoting the economic and political interests of the United States itself. It has long reflected U.S. values, however imperfectly. Promoting human rights, democracy, and development abroad and relieving the suffering of the needy are among those values.

Second are the increasing demands from African-Americans—10 percent of the U.S. population—that their country should maintain a presence and engagement in their ancestral part of the world. Signs of a heightened interest in Africa among African Americans include the creation of the Constituency for Africa and the African/African-American summits, among other activities. Also important is the growing influence of African Americans in U.S. politics, symbolized by a doubling in the numbers of African Americans in the 103rd Congress.

The American public, relieved of Cold War anxieties and absorbed with the country's numerous domestic problems, could always demand a mildly isolationist U.S. foreign policy, a "retrenched isolationism" as some have dubbed it. Early signs of the emergence of such a policy were evident in the Bush administration. But events beyond U.S. borders have already demonstrated the difficulty of sustaining that policy, with the intervention in Somalia—a country where the United States has almost no material interests—as the most telling example. Death and destruction there, captured by the electronic media and beamed into American homes, raised public concern and caught President George Bush's attention as he prepared to leave the White House. Pressures for U.S. intervention strengthened when relief organizations threatened to abandon Somalia if better security was not provided and when other governments and international institutions proved unable or unwilling to put an end to the unfolding tragedy.

The problem of Somalia brings us to the first of three main issues confronting the United States in Africa today and into the twenty-first century. In the past two years, two African countries have been overwhelmed by civil conflict—Liberia and Somalia. Civil conflicts have continued in Sudan, Senegal, Mali, Niger, and Rwanda and have reemerged in Angola. Severe ethnic violence has broken out in Zaïre and Kenya, and renewed conflicts in Ethiopia and Mozambique cannot be ruled out. It was widely hoped that the end of the Cold War would also bring about resolution to many of the long-standing internal wars in Africa, especially those in which the United States and the Soviet Union had become involved. But this hope has been traduced. What has provoked these deadly conflicts? Are others likely to break out in the coming decade? And what can be done to resolve or avoid them?

Another important change in Sub-Saharan Africa over the past two years has been the adoption by one government after another of political reforms leading to more democratic governance. In nearly every country in the region, elections have been promised or held. In many countries, controls on the media have been reduced, and opposition political parties permitted. These are promising changes, but there is no guarantee that they will be extended or consolidated. What can the United States do to help Africans realize their aspirations for democratic government and political participation?

A re-examination of U.S. policies is also warranted given the economic crisis that has afflicted the region for over a decade, despite widespread and prolonged efforts at economic reform by most African governments and large inflows of foreign aid. Has the reform recipe failed or has it been inadequately tested? What else needs to be done to spur development in Africa? What role should U.S. policies play in this effort?

Answers to questions about U.S. policies in Africa must be sought with two facts in mind. First, the United States is only one of a number of foreign governments and international institutions involved in Africa. Washington cannot act alone on these issues and expect to be effective. It must act in concert with other governments, especially the French and British, and with international institutions—particularly the World Bank, the International Monetary Fund (IMF), the European Community, and the United Nations. Second, even though the United States is not the only foreign government active in Africa, its words and actions can still have a major influence over the way other foreign governments, international institutions, and Africans think and behave—if only because the United States is now the only great power and unencumbered by the baggage of a colonial past.

This essay is intended as a contribution to the discussion and debate that must take place in coming months and years on the future of U.S. policy in Africa.

Part II
Sub-Saharan Africa Today

■ AFRICA SOUTH OF THE SAHARA is a large and diverse region, with nearly all the world's climates and a wide range of mineral and agricultural resources. There, nearly 450 million Africans practice Islam, Christianity, and traditional African religions. Among the 47 independent states of Sub-Saharan Africa are 17 ministates, with populations of 3 million or less, 15 small states with populations of between 3 million and 10 million, 7 medium-size states with populations of 20 million or more, and one large state—Nigeria—with over 80 million inhabitants (Table 1). Fourteen small countries are landlocked. Some, especially in the Sahel, are poor both in natural resources and income.

Despite this great diversity, much of Sub-Saharan Africa shares a number of common social, political, and economic characteristics. Nearly every country but Liberia and Ethiopia experienced decades of colonial rule by European powers. Most African countries are multi-ethnic. Family, village, clan, and ethnic group provide an individual's fundamental source of identity and claim primary loyalty.

A number of countries, particularly those along the west coast of Africa and continuing across the continent through Chad, the Sudan, and Ethiopia, include large Moslem and Christian communities. Although these ethnic and religious divisions do not bring with them the historic hatreds and blood feuds so evident in parts of Eastern Europe, they do represent societal cleavages that can, if managed poorly by politicians, produce dangerous social tensions and conflict.

. . . .

POLITICAL PATTERNS OF DEVELOPMENT
1960–1990

■ ANOTHER PATTERN COMMON TO MUCH of Africa from the early 1960s just after independence until 1990 was the establishment of authoritarian political regimes. Most newly independent African countries inherited democratic political systems modelled on those of the former colonial power. These were quickly discarded and replaced by civilian dictators or military juntas. Typically, opposition political parties were banned, coopted, or harassed out of existence. The ruling party, often controlled from the top, was accountable mainly to the political leadership rather than the party membership or the people. The media was muzzled by government. Legislatures were turned into rubber stamps or discarded altogether. The independence of the judiciary was sometimes compromised, with presidents claiming the right not only to hire but also to fire judges, or to set up alternative judicial systems (for example, revolutionary or peoples' courts). Sometimes the executive simply bypassed the courts by passing preventative detention acts or declaring states of emergency. Private groups—youth, women, professional, unions, cooperatives—were brought under government or party control or banned altogether by Africa's autocrats. The typical political system in Africa by 1970 was one of "personal rule"—leadership by an individual supported by a coterie of followers and often unrestrained by the rule of law or public or private institutions.[2]

Political leaders maintained themselves in power in several ways: they provided their supporters with patronage through access to state resources, including jobs, foreign travel, opportunities for rent-seeking, access to bank loans (often unsecured and not intended to be repaid), government contracts, and a host of other advantages.

Another element in regime maintenance in Africa was the promise by political leaders to bring rapid development to their peoples. Many an African autocrat argued that progress would be more easily achieved if the time-consuming debates and negotiations typical of democratic systems were avoided and if the state could make and implement development policies quickly. In an implicit social contract between the leaders and the masses, the latter effectively exchanged their political rights for their leader's promise of rapid improvement in their economic situation.

Many African leaders sought to legitimize themselves with their peoples and their neighbors in another way—by pointing to their status abroad, including membership in the United Nations and, above all, close relationships with non-African powers. State visits to major world capitals; large and increasing amounts of economic aid from foreign governments; treaties of friendship with the Soviet Union; and participation in the commonwealth meetings, Franco-African summits, and other multilateral organization or international conferences all served this purpose.

Finally, African autocrats repressed opposition. Harassment, arrest, torture, exile, and assassination were not the instruments of choice

TABLE 1. PROFILE OF SUB-SAHARAN AFRICA

Country	Population 1991 (millions)	GNP Per Capita 1990 ($)	GDP Growth (percent) 1986-89[a]	GDP Growth (percent) 1990
Angola	10.3	na	7.1	na
Benin	4.9	360	0.2	3.9
Botswana	1.3	2,230	11.5	5.7
Burkina Faso	9.3	330	2.7	1.3
Burundi	5.6	210	4.1	3.6
Cameroon	12.1	960	−6.1	−2.5
Cape Verde	0.4	680	6.6	2.1
Central African Republic	3.1	390	0.4	0.7
Chad	5.8	180	6.9	0.7
Comoros	0.5	480	1.1	0.8
Congo (People's Republic)	2.4	1,000	1.2	1.0
Côte d'Ivoire	3.6	750	−1.3	−2.6
Djibouti	0.4	na	0.3	1.2
Equatorial Guinea	0.4	340	3.3	3.1
Ethiopia	53.0	120	4.0	−1.6
Gabon	1.2	3,550	−0.9	4.7
Gambia, The	0.9	340	4.2	1.5
Ghana	15.3	390	5.1	3.0
Guinea	5.9	440	4.8	4.1
Guinea-Bissau	1.0	180	5.9	3.0
Kenya	25.0	370	5.6	4.3
Lesotho	1.8	540	10.2	4.4
Liberia	2.6	na	na	na
Madagascar	12.0	230	2.9	3.0
Malawi	8.8	200	3.2	4.7

TABLE 1. CONTINUED

Country	Population 1991 (millions)	GNP Per Capita 1990 ($)	GDP Growth (percent) 1986-89[a]	1990
Mali	8.7	280	1.5	3.4
Mauritania	2.0	500	3.4	−1.5
Mauritius	1.1	2,310	9.5	5.3
Mozambique	16.1	80	5.5	1.9
Namibia	1.8	1,080	na	na
Niger	7.9	310	0.1	3.1
Nigeria	99.0	290	5.1	5.7
Rwanda	7.4	310	−1.9	−1.7
São Tomé and Principe	0.1	400	0.8	2.5
Senegal	7.6	710	2.7	4.5
Seychelles	0.1	4,820	4.9	6.6
Sierra Leone	4.2	250	3.4	3.0
Somalia	8.0	na	1.2	−1.6
South Africa	36.8	2,530	−4.3	na
Sudan	25.8	400	1.0	−1.5
Swaziland	0.8	1,030	6.5	9.8
Tanzania	25.3	na	4.6	4.1
Togo	3.8	410	3.6	−0.5
Uganda	16.9	na	9.0	4.3
Zaïre	38.5	220	0.4	−1.9
Zambia	8.4	420	2.9	−1.4
Zimbabwe	10.1	650	na	na

[a]Average annual percentage change.
Source: Adapted from *African Social and Economic Trends, 1992 Annual Report* (Washington, DC: The Global Coalition for Africa, 1992) Tables 1.1, 1.7, and 5.1.

of most African leaders for protecting their political positions. But most were prepared to use them when they judged their positions threatened.

There were exceptions to authoritarian rule in Africa during the three decades following 1960. Botswana, the Gambia, and Mauritius all maintained relatively open political systems during this period although only in Mauritius did government change hands as a result of elections. After 1974, the Senegalese government permitted opposition political parties to form. Nigeria, Ghana, and several other countries alternated between democratic elections and military coups. The one-party states of Kenya (under Jomo Kenyatta) and Tanzania allowed a measure of political competition in their elections. But, until 1990, these were the exceptions, not the rule.

. . . .
ECONOMIC TRENDS SINCE THE 1960s

■ IN ADDITION TO COMMON SOCIAL AND political characteristics, African economies have also followed a similar pattern. At independence, three-quarters or more of Africans were employed in agricultural production, mostly as small farmers utilizing low input technologies. Little has changed over the past three decades.

The economies of African states, now as then, rely on one or two primary export commodities: food, beverages, fibers, and minerals. They still import most of their manufactured goods, industrial inputs, capital goods, and an increasing volume of food. Another pattern in African economies has been the gradual expansion of state intervention through nationalizations; through the imposition of regulations governing labor practices, investment, international trade, and internal commerce; and through controls on prices, interest rates, and wages. Many of these policies of government expansion and control were an outgrowth of deliberate strategies. Others were ad hoc responses to the economic instability of the 1970s when export prices tumbled and governments dealt with scarcities in foreign exchange, imported goods, and credit by price controls and rationing.

By the beginning of the 1980s, the thrust of economic policies in most of Sub-Saharan Africa involved a resource transfer from rural agricultural producers to urban consumers and the public sector. The resources were extracted through a variety of taxes, price controls, and exchange-rate overvaluation. They were used to finance rapidly expanding government wage bills and to subsidize the prices of staples, including food and transport. Ceilings on food prices reduced farm income but boosted the income of urban consumers. Overvalued exchange rates depressed the prices farmers received for their produce while benefiting urban consumers by keeping down the prices of the imported goods which they consumed.[3]

Economic growth had been slowing since 1960, but the 1970s and 1980s brought real economic hardship to Sub-Saharan Africa. Export earnings fell as the volume of exports of many African countries declined and as world market prices dropped. Import costs rose as petroleum prices soared in the 1970s, igniting inflation in the West. Agricultural growth slowed as government taxing and price policies discouraged increased production. Population pressure brought marginal lands into cultivation and reduced fallow periods (and so soil fertility) on already cultivated land. Industrial production plummeted as the shortage of foreign exchange choked off vital imports of spare parts and raw materials. Foreign debt soon proved unserviceable.

One African government after another turned to their foreign creditors for debt rescheduling and increased aid. Before agreeing to give more aid or to reschedule debt, the creditors—commercial banks and governments—required African states to adopt both a stabilization program approved by the International Monetary Fund and a structural adjustment program approved by the World Bank. In 1977, only seven African countries had entered into stabilization programs with the IMF. By 1983, 15 countries had adopted such programs. And by 1992, 33 African nations were participating in IMF stabilization programs. These programs typically included a currency devaluation (except in franc-zone countries), reductions in government budgetary deficits, and restrictions on new credit. These policies were supposed to make gaps in the balance of payments manageable, primarily by restraining domestic demand. Once an economy had been stabilized, investment was expected to rise and growth to resume.

This anticipation proved false. Balance-of-payments gaps were often narrowed, but by less than expected and only temporarily. The benefits of reforms were often overwhelmed by the effects of adverse external shocks—like a collapse in export prices. New investment failed to appear. Indeed, the demand-restraint policies encouraged by the IMF depressed investment instead of increasing it, and many African economies continued to stagnate in the 1980s. At this point, the World Bank began to gain prominence in lending for structural adjustment in Africa.

World Bank lending to support economic reform in Africa actually began in 1979 with its first structural adjustment program in Senegal. Structural adjustment programs differed from stabilization programs in two ways: 1) Their goal was to promote long-term growth rather than simply to close the gap in the balance of payments; and 2) the scope of potential reforms contained in such programs was broad, including everything from rehabilitation of transport systems, to reorganizing or eliminating government agencies, investment, trade, and labor codes, to restructuring the health and educational systems. Structural adjustment programs were supported by relatively large loans, usually on highly concessional terms to the many poor countries of Sub-Saharan Africa. By the mid-1980s, macroeconomic reform programs were supplemented increasingly with smaller sectoral adjustment reform programs from the World Bank, the United States, and other aid donors. By 1992, few African countries had not had a stabilization, structural adjustment, or sectoral adjustment program with one or both of the Bretton Woods institutions.

Many African governments adopted their first economic reform programs in the first half of the 1980s, but the most intensive period of reform occurred in the second half of the decade. By the late 1980s, some promising signs of economic recovery appeared in a number of countries implementing reform programs. However, private investment—the key element in the long-term success of these economic reform programs and the anticipated engine of future economic growth—remained limited throughout the region.

. . . .
FIRST STEPS TOWARD POLITICAL LIBERALIZATION

■ THE WEAKNESS OF ECONOMIC recovery in Africa and the worsening problems in some countries, despite nearly a decade of reforms, fueled deepening economic discontent on the part of urban workers and

civil servants. These groups, among the more influential in African societies, had seen their standards of living fall as a consequence of economic
reforms. Their cost of living had risen as their salaries were frozen or
reduced; and some had lost their jobs. Their discontent became manifest
by the end of the decade with strikes, riots, and demonstrations against
deteriorating economic conditions and new austerity measures. These
demonstrations soon turned into demands for political reform. The lessons
of political changes in Eastern Europe, often a direct result of public
pressures and demonstrations, were not lost on Africans who saw what
a discontented, aroused public could do against authoritarian regimes.
Naturally they reasoned, "If political change is possible in Eastern Europe
and even in South Africa, why not in the rest of Africa?"

Autocrats, often unsure of their control of the military or the
willingness of their troops to shed blood to protect their regimes, began
to give way in the face of public demands. In Benin 1990, President
Mathieu Kerekou called a "national conference" of Beninese from a wide
variety of professions and political persuasions to rewrite the country's
constitution. He got more than he bargained for: the conference not only
rewrote the constitution to ensure a separation of powers and reduce
executive controls, but also stripped Kerekou of many of his responsibilities, set dates for a referendum on the new constitution and elections for
municipal and national officials, established a transition government, and
elected an interim prime minister. Demands for a national conference
were soon heard in other countries of Francophone Africa, and such
conferences were held in Mali, Niger, Congo, Togo, Zaïre, and Gabon.
Not all of them created wholly new political institutions or new governments but all contributed to a measure of political opening in each of
their countries.

In the first two years of the 1990s, political liberalization also
picked up momentum in Portuguese- and English-speaking Africa. Elections were held in Cape Verde, São Tomé and Principe, and Zambia, and
new governments were installed. Constitutions were revised to permit
multiparty politics in Kenya, Tanzania, Sierra Leone, Burkina Faso, Cameroon, and the Central African Republic. Elections were promised in
Nigeria, Kenya, Guinea, Gabon, Madagascar, Togo, and a number of
other countries.

However, not all governments moved toward politically open systems, and not all elections were free and fair. The elections in 1992 in Cameroon, Ghana, and Kenya, in which sitting presidents were reelected, were widely regarded as marred by irregularities and vote fraud. The Angolan political party and guerrilla movement, UNITA (União Nacional para a Independência Total de Angola), defeated in the first round of the elections which were generally regarded as fair, was unwilling to accept its loss and soon returned to the bush to restart the civil war. The Nigerian government had to postpone presidential elections, set for December 1992, to June 1993 because of extensive vote fraud during party primaries. By the end of 1992, the spread of democracy in Africa appeared to be slowing.

. . . .

MARGINALIZATION OF AFRICA

■ IF ECONOMIC AND POLITICAL conditions in Africa were changing in uncertain directions, the world beyond the continent had also changed dramatically with important implications for the Africans. Michael Clough, in his book, *Free at Last,* remarks that "The Cold War ended in Africa on December 28, 1988, with the signing of a tripartite agreement clearing the way for the independence of Namibia, Africa's last colony, and the withdrawing of Cuban troops from Angola."[4] In fact, the signs that the Soviet Union was unwilling to acquire any new African clients were evident by the beginning of the 1980s when Soviet officials rejected an appeal from the government of Ghana for aid to help them avoid having to turn to the IMF. Moscow reportedly advised the Ghanaians to negotiate with the IMF anyway. Mozambique and Ethiopia were turned down for membership in the Council for Mutual Economic Assistance. Internal Soviet policy discussions from the beginning of the 1980s reportedly included increasingly insistent voices that Moscow limit its engagement in Africa.[5] By the end of the decade, Soviet officials were warning Ethiopia that their aid could not continue. By 1991, the Soviet Union no longer existed, and the Russian Republic had begun to close embassies in Sub-Saharan Africa, including Togo, Niger, Sierra Leone, Burkina Faso, Somalia, Liberia, and Chad.

With the end of the Cold War and the breakup of the Soviet Union, Western governments began to reassess their presence in Africa. The limited interests that the United Kingdom and Germany had in many African countries and the poor economic performance of most of those countries led the British government to begin closing embassies in Africa (including those in the Congo, Gabon, and Liberia) and the Germans to consider closing some of theirs. Overall aid flows to African countries, after average increases of 4 percent a year in the 1980s, began to stagnate in the early 1990s. Some donors—for example, Italy and the Arabs—began to slash their aid to Africa.[6] France—the principal foreign economic partner of most of Francophone Africa—remained deeply engaged militarily, economically, and diplomatically in the region. However, a rising tide of criticisms from within France of its African policies and the problems of maintaining the franc zone (on which, more in Part III) may presage the beginning of a change in the level of French engagement in Africa.

The "marginalization of Africa" is not just speculation. Not only are foreign governments closing embassies and cutting back aid flows, but Africa's role in the world economy is also shrinking. African exports and imports as a percentage of total world trade contracted from 4 percent in 1965 to 2 percent in 1992.[7] Sub-Saharan Africa is seen less and less as a credible or useful economic and diplomatic partner and increasingly as a humanitarian problem for the world.

Part III
Three Key African Challenges

CIVIL CONFLICT

■ DURING THE THREE DECADES of independence, conflict has beset Africa, but rarely has one African country attacked another. Most of the conflicts have been internal—protests by discontented groups and political movements (often based on ethnic allegiances) challenging governments for power. Major internal wars in Africa have included civil wars in Nigeria, Ethiopia, Uganda, Chad, and Mozambique. Civil strife in Sudan, Angola, Liberia, and Somalia is still under way. And Togo and Zaïre appear close to a breakdown in law and order, and an insurgency by discontented Tuareg tribesmen continues in several Sahelian countries.

The end of the Cold War prompted hope that conflicts in Africa would diminish as the great powers withdrew their support from warring parties. To some extent, this hope has been realized. The termination of Soviet economic and military support for the Mengistu government in Ethiopia hastened the toppling of that regime and the end of its war with Eritrea and other domestic forces. The great powers cooperated to bring about a cease-fire and peace agreement in Angola, though this agreement has not held. The end of the Cold War may have helped indirectly bring about a peace agreement between the warring factions in Mozambique, as FRELIMO (Frente da Libertacão de Moçambique) realized that the Soviet Union would no longer provide military and economic support. If Mozambique, already increasingly dependent on foreign aid to survive, was to receive significant and sustained economic support, it would have to accommodate to Western pressures to democratize and negotiate with RENAMO (Resistencia Nacional de Moçambique).

CAUSES OF CONFLICT BEYOND THE COLD WAR

The end of the Cold War has not, however, brought peace to Africa. First, most African states, whether authoritarian or democratic, remain fragile. Their weak public institutions preside over ethnically and religiously divided societies, often unable to constrain the abuse of power by political elites. And ethnic identity still takes precedence over national identity in most states. Where ethnic sensibilities are exploited or mismanaged by politicians, internal conflict can result.

Africans well know these dangers. Political leaders in authoritarian or one-party states, for example Cameroon or Tanzania, as well as in newly established democracies such as Benin, often make sure to include representatives of major ethnic groups in their cabinets—so much so that certain ministries come to be known as representing specific ethnic groups. The equivalent of affirmative action programs govern civil service hiring and promotions in some countries, for example, Nigeria, to ensure that no one ethnic group predominates. Political parties in many countries are required to establish offices and have members from every region of their countries to avoid becoming earmarked as the parties of particular ethnic groups. These rules are not always fully effective. Although many parties remain ethnically or regionally based, the restrictions do at least extend their constituency bases and help to blur the ethnic implications of political competition.

Where social diversity has been abused and poorly managed, conflict has eventually erupted. Nearly all of Africa's internal wars have arisen from attempts by one ethnic group or alliance of groups to exclude others from power and access to state resources or from their attempts to assimilate or repress other groups. The civil war in Nigeria arose out of Ibo discontent and fear of exclusion and violence from other ethnic groups in Nigeria. The war in Ethiopia arose after Emperor Haile Selassie, contrary to his promises and the wishes of the Eritreans, extinguished the region's autonomy within the Ethiopian empire.[8] The war in Sudan has resulted from efforts by the Arabic-speaking northerners to impose Moslem Sharia law on the Shulik or Nilotic peoples of the south who are Christians or practice traditional religions. The war in Angola also has a strong ethnic element, with UNITA representing primarily Ovimbundus and the MPLA (Movimento Popular para Libertacão de Angola) drawing its support primarily from mestizos. Liberia erupted after years of autocratic rule by President Samuel Doe, who favored his ethnic group, the Krahns, and excluded the Krus, Gios, Manos, and others. The Krus, Gios, and Manos make up the main base of support for Charles Taylor whose army has fought for power in Liberia over the past several years. The conflict in Somalia arose out of former president Siad Barre's favoring his clan, the Marehan, and excluding or repressing others.

The potential for ethnic conflict exists in Togo and Zaïre, where opposition forces continue to pressure Presidents Eyadèma and Mobutu and their supporters (often drawn from their family, ethnic group, or region) to surrender power. The Togolese military, made up mainly of Kbaye people, a minority ethnic group to which Eyadèma belongs, has used violence against those demanding democratic changes in Togo and this, in turn, has increased hostility and violence against the Kbaye. In Zaïre there have already been incidents of violence in the southern Shaba province against people coming from other parts of the country. Ethnic violence has broken out recently in Kenya, accompanying political party organization and competition. (Many observers believe the Kenyan government provoked or at least acquiesced to that violence as a means of proving its contention that multipartyism would lead to ethnic conflict.) The Oromos, the largest ethnic group in Ethiopia, have threatened to turn to violence to gain "their share" of political power in the new government. Ethnic violence appears to be growing in South Africa as the African National Congress, a large proportion of whose members are Xosha, and the Zulu-based Inkatha movement continue to maneuver for political position in the negotiations on a post-apartheid constitution.

Once a group becomes willing to fight a sitting government, it must find the resources to finance its war. This has usually meant a search for foreign patrons. For their own reasons, the great powers at times chose to support one side or another in these conflicts. Although that support has largely vanished with the end of the Cold War, other outside powers are still prepared to support factions in internal African wars. Libya is well known to be helping Charles Taylor in Liberia. It is believed that the Iraqis supported the government in Khartoum in its war against the south before the Gulf War. Iran is now thought to be financing the Islamic fundamentalist government in Khartoum as well as one of the warlords in Somalia. Kenya is also believed to be bankrolling one of the Somali warlords. Although non-African countries appear to be the principal sources of foreign government intervention in internal wars today, this is not always the case. South Africa long financed RENAMO in Mozambique, and the government of Uganda is widely believed to have had a role in supporting the invasion of Rwanda by disgruntled Tutsi exiles. Africans living abroad with ties to a warring faction have also financed conflicts. Eritrean guerrilla leaders tapped prosperous expatriates in Europe and the United States to finance the activities of the Eritrean Peoples Liberation Front. Prosperous Somalis in the United States and Italy are believed to be financing one warlord or another back home.

Thus, the foreign intervention so important to conducting wars and continuing them over long periods has not ended with the end of the Cold War. Indeed, with the elimination of Soviet involvement in African affairs and the decline in U.S. interest in the region, opportunities have increased for intervention by other governments in African conflicts. The great powers are now no longer willing to exert influence to exclude other powers from areas where they have had significant interests.

THE COLD WAR LEGACY

It is striking that the three countries where civil conflicts have become the most destructive—Somalia, Liberia, and Sudan—all had close relations with the United States before the outbreak of war, which may have played an indirect role in these wars. First, Washington had earlier strengthened these governments through generous military and economic aid, largely for diplomatic and strategic purposes. It wanted to reward President Numeiri of Sudan for supporting the Camp David Accords and to ensure a government friendly to Egypt on that country's southern border. It supported Siad Barre in Somalia because he agreed to provide the U.S. Rapid Deployment Force (created in response to the 1979 Soviet invasion of Afghanistan) with access to the port of Berbera in the event of an emergency in the Indian Ocean or the Middle East. Somalia also occupied a strategic position at the entrance of the Red Sea in a region that—in the mid-1970s—seemed to be turning increasingly toward the Soviets. The United States supported the Doe government in Liberia, knowing that Doe was probably incompetent and certainly corrupt, to dissuade him from establishing close relations with Libya and to protect U.S. communications assets.

The United States ignored growing human rights abuses and political mismanagement in each of these countries as well as in Zaïre (in the throes of an economic collapse of extraordinary proportions). Indeed, Washington may have inadvertently encouraged abuses through its symbolic political support of these governments with foreign aid, by receiving their leaders at the White House, and by extending other visible forms of cooperation. African leaders have often used the approbation associated with these forms of cooperation—particularly economic and military aid— as a means of legitimizing themselves with their peoples and their neighbors and intimidating potential opposition at home.

Foreign aid may also have eased pressures on these governments and their leaders to deal responsibly with their economies. While the United States attempted to link the level of its aid to needed economic reforms during the 1980s, Mobutu, Doe, Barre, and others knew that their aid would not be terminated if they ignored their promises to implement reforms—which most of them did. Aid for reform was a game and they had the upper hand.

In a more positive vein, the aid undoubtedly put some constraints on the human rights behavior of African leaders—at least for a time. Gross abuses of human rights would have produced strong pressures in Congress to reduce or eliminate U.S. aid, and African political leaders knew it. However, the aid was not used to persuade African leaders to avoid excluding significant proportions of their populations from power, making eventual internal conflict inevitable. When violence against these regimes did break out, Doe and Barre responded with even greater violence and repression.

By the time civil conflict was widespread or political breakdown pervasive, it was hard for external powers to intervene to restore order or broker lasting peace agreements. In any event, the United States no longer had much interest in these countries. The Cold War was over and their value, based largely on strategic considerations, was much diminished. Washington's attention was turned elsewhere, and there was no desire to become involved in the demanding, complex, risky, and almost surely costly efforts to resolve internal conflicts in these benighted countries. No other external power or regional hegemon was able or willing to act to ensure internal and political security in and among African states. This is the situation today.

. . . .

DEMOCRATIZATION

■ BY THE END OF 1992, nearly every Sub-Saharan African country had begun to implement political reforms. Most governments had changed their policies or constitutions to permit the formation of opposition political parties. Press freedom had been greatly expanded. Unions had begun to sever their ties with governments, and there had been a flowering of new associational groups throughout most of the region. Presidential and legislative elections had been held in roughly 20 countries and were scheduled in several others. In Cape Verde, Benin, Congo, Mali, Zambia, and several other countries, new governments had taken office.

THE SHAPE OF DEMOCRACY IN AFRICA

Political change is in the air throughout Africa, but it is important to be realistic about the nature of Africa's new democracies or partially liberalized regimes. Even in those countries where political liberalization has been the most extensive—for example, Benin or Zambia—the new regimes are still very different from Western-style democracies.

First of all, the newly established political institutions are weak and their rules of operation not yet fully elaborated. The true extent of an executive's powers and the limits placed on those powers by legislatures and judiciaries must be discovered over time. The organization and financing of legislatures and other organs of government remain a challenge—where salaries for legislators are small, only a few of the wealthy can afford to claim such positions. Where the salaries are generous, they can become a drain on government budgets already under severe stress. A strong and independent judiciary also requires funding and adequate training for its judges. An independent media needs to be financed (advertisements cannot serve as an adequate source of financing for African media), and journalists often lack training in their craft as well as in the substantive areas they are cover.

Second, the nature of political competition in Africa is much different from political competition in Western democracies and is likely to remain so for some time. Political parties are not based on class interests and seldom have distinct ideological visions and policy orientations, whatever their official rhetoric. Rather, they revolve around an individual political leader and are based on personal or ethnic ties, often reinforced with patronage (where parties gain power) or hopes of patronage.

From time to time, a coalition of opposition movements combines to challenge a sitting government, as in Zambia where the Movement for

Democratic Process (MDP) defeated former President Kenneth Kaunda and his United National Independence Party (UNIP). These opposition movements often find it difficult to cooperate, and where they form coalition parties, they sometimes prove unstable and fragmented once power is attained.

The associational groups, so familiar in Western democracies, which promote the interests of their members, are also weak and, until recently, few. Groups such as producer or professional organizations have begun to mushroom in many countries. But like political parties, they are often the personal followings of ambitious individuals. Time will tell whether they turn into genuine grassroots-based organizations wielding political influence or whether they will wither away. Meanwhile, they do not yet provide a basis for a coalition of interests on which Western political parties are frequently centered, nor are they yet able to act as a buffer and intermediary between government and the general public. For example, the few farmers' groups that exist in Africa tend to represent the interests of a handful of commercial farmers. Business interests, often organized in chambers of commerce, are, for the most part, limited and lacking in influence. Unions in many countries have only recently broken away from government control and are still adjusting to their role as independent organizations and to the difficulties of financing themselves and avoiding fragmentation.

One key question is whether the mass of African farmers, often making up three-quarters of a country's population, will claim a voice in the more open political systems of Africa today. In the past, they have had little influence, but the new democracies give them an opportunity to organize and act to protect their interests. Whether and how they act will be important both to the future of democracy and economic reform in Africa. Protecting more open political systems where their voices can be heard is very much in their interest. It is also important to the many farmers who grow export crops that their governments maintain economic reforms promoting those exports. Those reforms should also be protected because expanding agricultural production is key to healthy future growth in most of Africa. A few signs of a political awakening have appeared in rural areas, for example in Mali among cotton farmers. But in most of the region political parties or interest-based associations have not yet begun to form to represent small farmer interests.

Finally, the intangible element of "political culture" differentiates most African countries from Western democracies. Political culture is a term that is difficult to define precisely but refers to the key values and attitudes that influence a community's political behavior. These include willingness to abide by formal rules of political competition to tolerate dissenting views, to take political initiatives, to cooperate with others, and to compromise on issues of political disagreement. Africans frequently express fear that their years of repressive authoritarian regimes have created a political culture of intolerance and resistance to compromise that will undermine democracy.

Assessing the influence of past experience on African attitudes toward new democratic regimes is difficult, but the key question is not so much about the nature of their political culture as about how rapidly it can change. It was long thought that the experience of the Spanish under the authoritarian government of General Franco, combined with aspects of their culture such as hierarchical social organization and a tradition of individualism, would inhibit the consolidation of democracy there. That it did not suggests that political culture can change quickly. The extensive publicity given to the debates in national conferences, political campaigns, and elections in a number of African countries may have helped to educate Africans in democratic political practices and to reshape their political culture.

The nature of political institutions in Africa suggests that democracies there are likely to function differently from democracies in the West. These regimes are more open than their authoritarian predecessors, but their accountability to their publics remains weak. It will take time for an undertrained and underfinanced media to play the role it does in much of the West of putting issues on the national agenda, contributing to national debate, and investigating and criticizing government policy failures or corruption. The public may remain politically inert except at elections; even then, many Africans continue to base their votes on cues from village "big men" or ethnic brokers rather than on the government's performance. Governments will still maintain their support coalitions through patronage, and corruption is unlikely to disappear. All of these practices are evident in one or another of Africa's few long-surviving democracies.

There are several possible scenarios for the future pattern of politics in Africa. We may see for some time in Africa, assuming democracy is extended and consolidated, *de facto* one-party states where the principal political party remains in power without a serious electoral threat to its survival except during sustained crisis where widespread public discontent leads to an opposition alliance. Although this type of clientist democracy may neither look like Western democracies nor achieve the degree of competence, accountability, or probity that is common in Western political systems, it would represent a considerable improvement over the authoritarian governments of the past. If it endures, it is far more likely than Africa's autocracies to preserve human and civil rights, to mediate internal conflicts before they become violent, and to strengthen the rule of law.

In another scenario, the new political institutions may fail to function. The political parties (including the governing party) and associational groups may fragment, eventually paralyzing government decision-making. Fragmentation was one of the main problems behind the failure of Somalia's democratic experiment between 1960 and 1969.

Another rather different scenario is a concentration of power in the hands of a patronage-dispensing executive, and a concomitant weakening of legislative, judicial, and media independence. Extensive corruption is likely to go with such power, ultimately destroying the legitimacy of the government.

A fourth scenario involves the intrusion of ethnic hostilities into politics, as parties come to be identified with particular ethnic groups and the contest for power is perceived as a zero-sum game.

Several of these scenarios would likely end with a civilian or military coup d'état and the demise of democratic political institutions—in effect, leading to a re-creation of the authoritarian regimes of the past and possibly a pattern of alternation between elected civilian governments that prove weak, incompetent, or corrupt and military governments (which typically take power promising elections and a return to civilian rule). Already familiar in Ghana and Nigeria, this pattern could easily spread to other Sub-Saharan African countries.

None of these scenarios is predestined. Whether they occur or not will be the result of several factors. Among the most important will be the quality, skill, and commitment of the political leadership in individual countries, including not just the executives but also the legislators, the leaders of political parties, associational groups, and the military. Leaders who pander to ethnic loyalties will encourage conflict and destroy their democracies. Political party bosses out of power and unwilling to play by the rules of democratic governance may provoke repression, limit civil rights, or stage a civilian coup d'état. Leaders more interested in lining their pockets than guiding their countries toward healthy growth will undermine the legitimacy of their governments.

Public support will also play a role in influencing the extension and consolidation of democracy in Africa. If individual citizens remain actively supportive of democracy and willing to oppose efforts by government to curtail liberties or threats of military intervention, political leaders will be less willing to trample on civil rights and more willing to extend them. The military is committed (at least temporarily) to staying out of politics in a number of countries of the region and may remain so where they anticipate public opposition to their overturning elected governments.

Social characteristics of individual African societies will also play a role in preserving democratic government. Where social cleavages are sharp and lead to violence (between fundamentalist Moslems and evangelical Christians in Nigeria, for example), governments may feel they have no alternative but to resort to repression and limiting civil rights. Where societies exhibit strong tendencies toward factionalism, as in Somalia, the challenge of effective democratic governance may prove insuperable.

The characteristics of political institutions and electoral rules can play a role in minimizing or exacerbating ethnic politics or tendencies toward factionalism. However, deciding in advance which set of rules in a democratic system is most appropriate to a country's social characteristics is not always easy. A society in which many disparate groups demand a political voice might want elections based on proportional representation so that no significant group will feel excluded. It is now widely recognized that winner-take-all elections in Angola may have further provoked Jonas Savimbi and UNITA—who lost the election but retained their arms—to resume the civil wars. Paradoxically, proportional representation can also encourage factionalism and lead to political paralysis.

An increasingly influential factor in democracy's extension and consolidation in Africa involves the communications revolution. Africa received reports of public demonstrations in Eastern Europe against authoritarian governments, encouraging Africans to demand their civil rights. Even more influential, especially in Francophone Africa, were the pictures of Beninese criticizing past government abuse and debating political reforms during their national conference. This conference was broadcast on radio and television and was eagerly watched in neighboring countries. (Later the Congolese broadcast their national conference live on television. A major part of the audience was in Kinshasa, Zaïre, and it was not long before Zaïrois began to demand their own national conference.) Of course, the communications revolution can also have a negative impact. For instance, a successful military coup against an elected government in one country could set off coup attempts in other countries.

Democratic trends are increasingly affected as well by external pressures. The larger the number of democratic regimes in Africa, the greater the regional pressure is likely to be against the military's seizing power in any one of them. Democratic regimes will understandably feel threatened by a military coup in a nearby country and may want to act together to discourage future coups. They may, for example, isolate military regimes diplomatically or even impose sanctions on usurpers as the Organization of American States did against Haiti.

Potentially more important than the regional reaction to military coups' upsetting elected governments are the reactions of major foreign powers and international lending institutions. Foreign governments have already played an important role in the moves toward political liberalization in Africa by giving verbal support to the protection of human and civil rights, by financing activities to strengthen democracy (for example, national conferences and training of election observers, political party organizers, and journalists), and by tying their aid to democratic reforms. In a number of African countries, foreign-government support has strengthened the governments' movements, already under way, toward political reforms or encouraged the political opposition to take bolder risks in demanding reforms. In a few countries, like Kenya, the reduction of aid forced the government to permit opposition parties to organize and to set a date for elections.

The World Bank's emphasis on good governance—often interpreted by Africans to mean more open political systems—and the Bank's active role in pressing for political reforms, as in Kenya and Malawi, have added to these pressures. Sustained external pressure for the extension and maintenance of democracy can play a critical role in discouraging a return to authoritarianism in Africa. But where influential external powers are inconsistent in their support for democracy, the effect can be negligible or even disastrous. The extensive violence in Togo during the past year is the most dramatic illustration of the impact of inconsistent policies by powerful foreign governments: external pressures simultaneously encouraged the opposition to demand reforms and the incumbent government to repress those demands with violence.

Added to all these factors is another of overriding importance to political outcomes: economic performance. In the past widespread discontent with the poor economic performance of Africa's authoritarian regimes was a major force for political reforms. The new regimes will also be judged by how well they do economically. Most newly elected governments have inherited serious economic problems along with political power. If problems are to be overcome, governments have to implement painful economic reforms. Many observers believe that democracy and economic development go together, that healthy development may be inhibited without democracy and the accountability, transparency, and rule of law that accompany it. This view has considerable currency in Washington, both among U.S. government personnel and World Bank officials. But realities in Africa are not so simple.

Many of the economic reforms African governments must implement directly threaten the interests of politically influential groups. The downsizing of public agencies attacks the interests of civil servants, often organized in unions and among the most influential groups in African societies. Reductions in government expenditures, usually involving decreases in wages or employment and the removal of subsidies on basic foodstuffs, hurt unions and their constituents—many of whom led the attack on authoritarianism. Deregulation, financial reforms, privatization of state-owned enterprises, and trade liberalization adversely affect political elites and reduce the government's dispensable pools of patronage. Although these changes make good sense from an economic standpoint, they reduce the new governments' ability to retain the support of key constituency groups and individuals.

In some ways, the Africans confront a classic catch-22 situation: they must stimulate economic growth if their regimes are to remain legitimate in the eyes of their peoples, and to spur that growth and the aid needed to help finance it, they must implement painful reforms that undermine their support among key constituencies. Where political turmoil is great enough, reforms can make the country ungovernable. To add to these dilemmas, positive results from the economic reforms are likely to take a long time to appear, further straining political stability.

Though difficult, these problems need not be insurmountable. Effective political leadership in explaining the need for reforms; a belief among government officials and the informed public that the reforms have been decided by their government not imposed from the outside[9]; the same strict discipline among senior government officials over their own spending that they expect of others; absence of corruption in government; and a sense of fairness about distributing economic adversity among all citizens are all vital if reforms are to be viewed as credible and legitimate. Careful packaging and pacing of reforms by Africans and the aid agencies advising them is important to avoid a simultaneous attack on the interests of a wide range of politically influential groups that might stimulate the creation of broad-based, anti-reform coalitions. Though too small to be more than symbolic, public programs to ease the social costs of adjustment on the poor as well as segments of the middle class (especially the newly unemployed) are important for a government to show that it cares about the impact of the reforms on its citizens. To sustain reforms over that long and uncertain period until the new investments, jobs, incomes, and growth are stimulated, the public needs a sense that the reforms are producing benefits even if those benefits do not accrue directly to them. The rehabilitation of schools, roads, or health centers, for example, provides that evidence. In short, economic reforms in new democracies may have to proceed in a more politically sensitive manner than they have in the past when most of Africa was governed by all-powerful autocrats.

. . . .
DEVELOPMENT

■   MANY COUNTRIES OF SUB-SAHARAN AFRICA are among the world's poorest, least developed, and slowest growing. Africa is the biggest developmental challenge to the global community today and is likely to remain so well into the twenty-first century. During every decade since the 1960s, economic growth has slowed in this part of the world while population growth has accelerated. As a result, many Africans' real incomes are no higher today than in 1960. World Bank officials project that even African countries that embark on the needed economic reforms will take 70 years to double their per capita incomes from $1 to $2 a day.

However, not all the economic news from Africa is gloomy. The average African in 1980 was healthier and far better educated than in 1960, lived longer, and could travel more easily because of a larger number of roads. By 1990 significant progress has been achieved in developing human resources and infrastructure, neither captured directly in national income statistics. Yet even this progress is being eroded by the failure of agriculture and industry to grow and generate the government revenues needed to maintain social services and infrastructure. The peculiar economic failure of many African countries might be termed "development (in education and health) without growth (in the key productive sectors)." This economic strategy has proven unsustainable.

IMPACT OF ECONOMIC POLICY REFORM

There is little controversy today about the causes of this failure. Volatile export prices in the 1970s, the decline in their terms of trade during part of the 1980s, and other international economic trends in the past two decades have often been adverse to African interests. Far more important, however, have been the policy and institutional failures of African governments. Policies have discouraged the growth of productive investment, and public institutions have proven unable to fulfill their responsibilities—from regulating private economic activities to delivering goods and services to producers and the rest of the public.

Economic policy reform was promoted as the solution to these problems by the community of aid donors and accepted by many African governments during the 1980s. The impact of these reforms on economic recovery and growth has varied. According to the most recent review of adjustment lending by the World Bank, in the "intensive adjustment lending" countries in Sub-Saharan Africa, real growth and exports' share in the domestic economy between 1986 and 1990 have recovered to their average levels during the 1970s.[10] However, savings and investment between 1986 and 1990 show a small increase above the depressed levels between 1980 and 1985, although they have not yet reached the higher levels of the 1970s.

However, the aggregate trends of the "intensive adjustment" countries may be misleading since their individual investment and savings performance is quite diverse. In Ghana, investment has been gradually rising since the late 1980s but reached only 8 percent of the gross domestic product (GDP) by 1990. Savings, though also growing, reached only 11 percent of GDP by 1990. In Guinea-Bissau, in contrast, gross domestic investment has followed a variable but downward trend since the latter half of the 1980s. Gross investment in Malawi reached 15 percent of GDP in 1990, down slightly from the previous year but only half its level in the 1970s. None of these levels of savings and investment is adequate to sustain healthy economic growth.[11]

Trends in investment are especially important in evaluating the impact of economic reforms. Increased investment—led, it is widely assumed, by the private sector—must occur if economic reforms are to return a country to a sustainable growth path. In Sub-Saharan Africa the expected increase in private investment has not yet occurred. Indeed, in some countries, investment has diminished, a source of continuing concern to both African officials and the foreign governments and international institutions helping them.

Why the investment response to economic reforms in Africa has lagged is an increasingly urgent question. One answer is that not enough economic reforms have been implemented to attract new investment, particularly in manufacturing. Development specialists talk about a "critical minimum" of reforms necessary to stimulate investment. Although a critical minimum is not entirely clear, key elements in stimulating new investment are removing market distortions and regulatory obstacles to investment, protecting property rights, and making credit available. Exchange-rate adjustments that leave domestic price controls or regulatory barriers in place will not produce the expected investment. Where a wide range of reforms have been implemented without reforming the financial sector and expanding domestic credit, new investment is likely to be small at best. Reforms involving exchange-rate adjustments and the removal of price controls are now widespread throughout much of Africa. The reform or removal of regulations inhibiting private investment (for example, prohibitions on firms firing employees) have tended to be implemented more slowly, and a number of countries are only beginning financial sector reforms. Financial sector reforms have also been hard to execute; only half of them were fully implemented in 1980 to 1990.[12]

ECONOMIES OF THE CFA

Countries in the Communauté Financière Africaine (CFA) franc zone have had particular difficulties implementing stabilization and structural adjustment programs. Since their independence, 13 African countries, all but one (Equatorial Guinea) former colonies of France, have participated in two monetary unions with France: one, among countries in West Africa; the other, among countries in Central Africa. Members of each group share a common currency, a common central bank, and common monetary policies. The French treasury guarantees the convertibility of their currency—the CFA franc—at a fixed rate to the French franc. Members place 60 percent of their foreign exchange reserves in the French treasury and agree to limits on the amount of credit they can create each year. France is a member of the two central banks along with the African members of the monetary unions.[13]

Monetary unions are rare among independent countries. Traditionally the perceived disadvantages of such unions have included the ceding of control by individual member states over their own monetary policies and the ensuing constraints on their fiscal policies, among the principal tools of economic management for any government. Advantages of these unions for their African members have been the facilitation of trade and investment through a convertible currency and low inflation rates, resulting from the limits on member governments' ability to expand domestic credit. Until the 1980s, most Westerners and African members of these unions regarded them as on balance benefiting their countries' economic health. Recognizing these benefits, Guinea, which left the monetary union in 1958, has asked to rejoin. Ghana, in a break with other

Anglophone African countries, has also reportedly asked to join. (Neither request has been granted.)

In recent years, however, the economic costs of the CFA zone have greatly increased. The decline in the Africans' terms of trade and the drop in the value of the U.S. dollar vis-à-vis the French franc have resulted in an overvalued CFA franc, by an estimated 25 percent (and by as much as 60 percent in the Côte d'Ivoire). This overvaluation has encouraged imports, discouraged exports and investment, prompted capital flight, and opened a gap in their balance of payments. France is also finding the zone more costly. Many of the African members have borrowed extensively from foreign banks, accumulating heavy debt burdens they can no longer repay. As a result, their foreign exchange reserves have diminished, and the government of France has reportedly had to pay out an estimated $1 billion a year to keep the franc zone solvent and help members service some of their external debts.[14]

The stabilization of these economies has become a crucial task if their growth is to resume. Yet, member states are prohibited from devaluing their currencies to help achieve that stabilization. So they have attempted to reduce the gap in their balance of payments by depressing domestic demand, primarily by reducing government expenditures. Since the main component of government expenditures is the wages of civil servants, they have tried to freeze hiring and reduce wage payments through attrition, as in Senegal, or through reduction in nominal wages, as in the Côte d'Ivoire. In neither case has it been politically possible for governments to depress wages, production costs, and prices enough to make their economies internationally competitive and close their balance-of-payments deficits. For example, the decrease in nominal wages in the Côte d'Ivoire produced strikes and riots that threatened the stability of the government itself.

Neither the government of France nor the African leaders of franc-zone countries want to devalue the CFA franc, though some African officials have appeared more sympathetic to the idea recently. Some argue that a devaluation will not cure the stabilization problem but rather set off a surge of inflation as prices for imported goods and their substitutes rise. Whether the rate of inflation is high or low and how long it endures also depends on governments' ability to control public expenditures and credit. It is widely recognized that devaluation without controls on government expenditures is not likely to be effective. Another argument—that devaluation will destroy the franc zone by eroding confidence in currency convertibility—seems extreme. A devaluation need not destroy the zone if it is done smoothly and achieves stabilization. Perhaps the most fundamental reasons that France and its African partners do not want to devalue the CFA franc are political: the zone and its currency, supported by France, have become symbols of continuing French engagement in Francophone Africa. And some African elites profit from their countries' overvalued currency.

The Africans have come to rely on Paris for security, aid, and international leadership. France has relied on its special relationship with a number of African countries and its implied ability to speak for them (and perhaps other developing countries) in international fora as one of the foundations for its claim to an important seat at the table of world politics, even though it is no longer a great world power. With the changes in European and world politics and the rising costs of maintaining their African relations, how long the French government will resist pressure to devalue the CFA franc is not clear. Senegal, Cameroon, and the Côte d'Ivoire are finding it impossible to service their external debts even to the World Bank; the government of France may feel forced to finance repayments to the Bank, further raising the costs of the franc zone. (In fact, it has already repaid a portion of Cameroon's debt to the Bank and has promised to finance debt repayments of the Côte d'Ivoire, if necessary.) A change in the CFA franc may not be far off.

ROADBLOCKS TO REFORM

If economic reforms are widely recognized as necessary to African countries' recovery and future growth, why have their governments hesitated or resisted implementing needed reforms? Economists often answer this question by citing "a lack of political will" on the part of African leaders. But this explains little. Why has political will been lacking when the need for reforms is so widely acknowledged?

First, the ideal of state-led growth with equity is still cherished by many Africans, although past policies based on this ideal have failed.

Similarly, many Africans remain skeptical about the private sector's ability to promote development and leery about side effects of privately led growth, for example, inequitable distribution of wealth and concentration of economic power in the hands of ethnic minorities or foreigners. The absence of a definitive structural adjustment success on the African mainland has left Africans with faith but not fact as their ideological basis for continuing with economic reforms.

Second, in almost all African societies the main beneficiaries of economic reforms—the producers of exports (mainly rural agriculturalists)—typically lack political influence with their governments. Conversely, the people who bear the costs of those reforms are among the most influential segments of African societies—the urban middle and working classes, including civil servants and business interests dependent on government protection and largesse to survive. Unlike many other developing regions, African societies typically lack a sizeable independent, formal business sector with the capital and experience to seize quickly the new opportunities opened up by the reforms. Where it exists, the business class is small and often perceives its interests to be threatened by reforms. Trade liberalization exposes them to foreign competition; removal of government regulations loosens their monopoly holds on domestic markets; and the reduction in government contracts and other public resources means a cut in revenues. There are many small businesses in the very large informal sectors typical of most African economies. But the owners of these businesses—who might benefit from economic reforms—rarely have a significant political voice. In effect, the political constituency for economic reforms has been weak in African countries while opponents reforms have been politically influential.

Why then, have *any* reforms been implemented? In large part, the answer is found in the dependence of African economies on foreign exchange and foreign aid. Governments trying to avoid a major compression in their imports have sought increased external assistance and debt relief. Since the beginning of the 1980s, most donor governments and public and private creditors have made IMF- and/or World Bank-approved economic reform programs conditions for both debt rescheduling and increased assistance. The Bretton Woods institutions thus wield considerable influence over economic policy choices by Africans in favor of economic reforms.

The politics of economic reform in Africa put reformers in a bind. The absence of a business class that takes advantage of opportunities opened up by the reforms means that the investment response to the reforms, the anticipated engine of future growth, will take a long time to develop. A definitive adjustment success in Africa that might convince Africans that the reforms will eventually bear fruit will therefore remain elusive for an uncertain period. Meanwhile, the influential domestic constituency needed to support reforms remains weak, and internal pressures to reverse or undermine reforms remain strong and sometimes successful.

A third set of roadblocks to successful economic reforms are the nonpolicy obstacles to investment and growth present in many African countries. The World Bank has identified one of them as a particular challenge: "governance," or the behavior of the political leadership and government officials toward the governed.[15] Widespread corruption and the absence of the rule of law have discouraged many private investors from risking their resources in African countries. Governance has undoubtedly been a serious problem for a number of countries, for example, Zaïre. But in many other Sub-Saharan countries, corruption is not so extensive and the rule of law not so weak that investors inevitably reject the possibilities of investing.

A number of other difficult problems have inhibited investment. Perhaps the most influential is the lack of confidence on the part of potential investors—domestic and foreign—in the maintenance of economic reforms and political stability in African countries. Thirty years of frequent political and economic changes have understandably made many people wary of risking their capital in manufacturing and other projects that take a long period of time to pay off. Africa's current wave of political changes, though welcome, has undoubtedly increased uncertainties about future policy directions.

Another impediment to investment and reform is rudimentary and poorly maintained infrastructure, even after three decades of expanding African roads, ports, bridges, airports, and communications facilities. Unreliable road and air travel and poor facsimile and phone communications in many African countries make doing business difficult and expensive. Ironically, the cuts in public expenditures often accompanying stabilization and structural adjustment programs hasten the deterioration in infrastructure and social services by forcing cutbacks in recurrent costs and public investment.

The disappointing investment response in reforming countries is due to the fact that a number of countries are so small, poor, limited in resource endowment, and early in stage of development that a significant increase in private investment (domestic or foreign) may be a very long time in coming regardless of policy reform efforts. Among this group are Mali, Niger, Chad, Burkina Faso, and Somalia. The best thing these countries could do for their development in the near term is export part of their burgeoning populations to richer regions of Africa, perhaps in the context of an economic union. In none of the eight experiments in economic integration under way in Africa at present, however, is there a free migration of labor. Most African governments have been reluctant to accept an influx of labor from neighboring countries, fearing such an influx will depress wages, create security problems, tax strained social services, and upset ethnic or religious balances. (Even in the Côte d'Ivoire, where migrant labor from Niger, Mali, and Burkina Faso has been welcomed in the past, migrants have become the object of increasing political criticism from Ivorians.)

For the smaller, poorer African countries unlikely to benefit from substantial private investment even where their economies are well managed, it is time to consider what additional measures might be undertaken to stimulate their growth. Certainly, a continuing effort to promote human resource development and infrastructure is important. Public institutions may also have to do more to promote development, both in these and other African countries where the private sector—especially in industry—remains weak. But here again, the problem of weak institutions arises and must first be addressed. Even in the "Asian tigers,"[16] rapid development, occurred as a consequence of the active role of government agencies in promoting national development, effectively pursuing what was, in effect, an "industrial policy." Effective state involvement in promoting economic development is likely to be even more important in poorer, less developed countries like those of Africa, where the private sector is also relatively undeveloped and likely to remain so. Development specialists urgently need to return to the question of how to strengthen Africa's public sector in promoting economic development.

A final, little recognized set of roadblocks to reform involves the challenges of increasing agricultural production. Expanding agricultural production is critical to Sub-Saharan Africa's economic recovery and future growth. The sector provides many countries with the bulk of their exports and food for their rapidly expanding populations. If agricultural production lags, export earnings decline and food import bills rise, putting a drag on economic growth. Further, an impoverished rural sector—where 8 out of 10 Sub-Saharan Africans still live—means that internal markets remain limited. Agricultural growth averaged 2.4 percent in Africa between 1986 and 1989, a small improvement over less than 1 percent rate between 1974 and 1985. But this growth came largely from putting more land under cultivation rather than increasing productivity on the land already being farmed.

Most African agriculture is "low input," utilizing simple tools, unimproved seeds, and little chemical fertilizer, and dependent on rainfall. Although the type of agriculture has been well adapted technically to a difficult physical environment, rapid population expansion is rendering it increasingly untenable. As the number of farmers increases, marginal lands are being farmed and the fallow periods needed for the soil to regain its fertility are being shortened. Soils have also been lost to erosion, and whole forests in a number of African countries have disappeared, victims of rural dwellers' firewood needs and of uncontrolled logging. As a result, agricultural yields have begun to decline in a number of countries and increases in aggregate output have failed to keep up with the 3 percent or more annual increase in population.

What is clearly required is the development and spread of viable technical packages that will enable African farmers to cultivate their land more intensively and more productively.

Crop yields in particular places have been improved without causing economic degradation and impairing future agricultural growth. The best known advance has been in export crops and in corn in the higher elevations of Kenya and in Zimbabwe. But the variability in soil, weather, and cultural conditions in Africa has prevented the major leaps forward in productivity like the Green Revolutions for wheat and rice that have so benefited Asia and Latin America.

Nevertheless, some of the international agricultural research centers working on African foodstuffs have come up with improvements in basic crop breeding. Still urgently needed, however, are the effective national research institutions and extension services that can adapt those improvements to local conditions and deliver them to African farmers. Many African countries have national agricultural research institutions and their governments have been no less generous in financing them than have governments elsewhere in the world relative to the size of their economies. Like so many public institutions in Africa, however, these institutions have proven weak, poorly managed, and unproductive. Development specialists must find a way to strengthen these institutions. This is no easy task since the reasons African public institutions in general have been so weak are poorly understood, despite the attention development practitioners have paid to the issue off and on for three decades.

Part IV
United States and Africa: Into the Twenty-First Century

RESOLVING CIVIL CONFLICTS

■   AT THE TOP OF THE AGENDA of U.S.-Africa relations must be
the development of policies to help prevent civil conflicts and to relieve
suffering and restore law and order where turmoil nonetheless occurs.
The Bush administration followed a policy of leaving conflict resolution
to the Africans. Sporadic and limited efforts were made by senior officials
of the State Department's Bureau of African Affairs to broker negotiations
among warring parties in some of these conflicts, as in Ethiopia, or to
encourage warring factions to stop fighting, as in Liberia and Angola.

The conflict in Somalia, ignored by Africa and most of the rest of
the world for so long, shows the limitations of a "hands-off" policy. This
unresolved civil conflict destroyed an economy, a society, and hundreds
of thousands of human lives. In the early period of turmoil in Somalia
(where the United States had supported the Siad Barre government for
15 years with economic and military aid), the United States was possibly
the only external power with enough credibility or clout to nudge the
government and Somali dissidents toward cooperation. The Italian government tried to broker a peace and failed. Somalia's neighbors, both in
the Horn of Africa and across the Red Sea in Arabia, made little effort
to mediate between the warring factions. And neither the Organization
of African Unity (OAU) nor the United Nations were willing or able to
intervene effectively to halt the approaching anarchy. Only when international nongovernmental organizations and the world media called attention to this human tragedy of terrific magnitude did an aroused public
demand that something be done to stop the dying.

If other tragedies like the one in Somalia are possible elsewhere
in Africa (and few doubt that they are), further armed humanitarian
intervention might become necessary, with the United States at times
the only power willing and able to do the job. It would be far less costly
in terms of African lives as well as American treasure for the United
States to act early to help resolve emerging conflicts. The United States
cannot, however, assume the role of permanent peacemaker or policeman
in Africa. It cannot act effectively without the support of its allies and it
cannot devote the resources or sustain the public support (at home or

abroad) such a role would require. Yet the United States could do much in the short run to promote peace and in the long run to establish mechanisms for conflict resolution.

A NEW U.S. CONFLICT RESOLUTION POLICY

The United States should adopt a two-track approach to African conflict: 1) help African governments deal with emerging internal conflicts in the near term; and 2) support efforts to increase the capacity of the OAU, the United Nations, or other appropriate multilateral organizations to assume that role in the long run. On both tracks, the United States must operate in a multilateral context. African leaders and other major governments with interests in the region—above all, France—must be involved and supportive if U.S. policies are to be effective.

The United States can take some direct and immediate actions to support peace in Africa's fragile states. Many of these are not new.

■ U.S. ambassadors should actively encourage African leaders publicly to address internal conflicts before they turn violent, to mediate the resolution of such conflicts that do break out;

■ Ambassadors should threaten to reduce or eliminate U.S. aid if government leaders ignore or exacerbate national conflicts, to discourage external powers from supporting one side or another in internal African conflicts, and to provide economic and military assistance to African governments in support of conflict resolution, including training military and police forces in handling demonstrations and insurgencies with a minimum of violence and bloodshed;

■ Washington-based officials must reinforce these initiatives—especially since over the past decade support from Washington for such initiatives has at times been ambiguous.

In some cases, no amount of external persuasion or pressure will keep conflicts from turning into civil wars. On many more occasions, a timely engagement by an influential outside power in helping governments to resolve conflicts will save lives and livelihoods.

What is suggested here need not be expensive in terms of U.S. staff or budgetary costs. A more activist policy will, however, require a measure of increased attention and effort by senior U.S. government officials in times of crisis. An administration that can and will focus on only one or two high priority foreign policy issues is not one that will pursue a more activist U.S. policy in Africa. However, we have already seen that ignoring internal African conflicts may prove far more costly— even for us—than attempting to resolve them before they turn bloody.

A second element in a U.S. policy of conflict resolution in Africa is supporting the creation of African and international norms and mechanisms for dealing with those conflicts in the future. One of the reasons that the United Nations and the OAU have been so slow to address problems of internal wars, like that of Somalia, is that international and African diplomatic norms have emphasized noninterference in the affairs of other countries, even where conflicts were severe. As the concept of national sovereignty is increasingly eroded and intractable internal conflicts more common, new internationally agreed norms should be established regarding when and how the world community and other nations should act to 1) mediate internal conflicts; 2) separate warring factions; 3) provide humanitarian relief in times of conflict; and 4) restore political order. It will not be easy or quick to develop such norms but an effort needs to be initiated immediately if the international community is to begin to assume the responsibility for dealing with these issues. In Africa, that effort may be spurred by the implicit threat of intervention by non-African powers in resolving African problems. Africans have already been embarrassed by the foreign intervention in Somalia.

Effective mechanisms for implementing established norms are needed. Such mechanisms might include the creation of an international or regional agency specializing in conflict resolution, and a U.N. or regional rapid deployment force or arrangements for quickly assembling such a force to intervene to halt fighting. The United States has the ability not only to suggest ideas regarding the nature of these new mechanisms (and so, to initiate international debates and prod decisions) but also to contribute part of the resources to help establish them. It may make sense for the administration to consider setting aside in the federal budget a line item or contingency fund to help finance the costs of international mediation and peacekeeping. Of course, the United States should first fulfill its existing financial obligations for past U.N. peacekeeping missions.

. . . .

SUPPORTING DEMOCRACY IN AFRICA

■ THE UNITED STATES MUST ACTIVELY support the process of democratization in Sub-Saharan Africa for three reasons. First, helping others achieve and protect their political rights has long been one of the key values in U.S. foreign policy, pre-dating Woodrow Wilson. This value has often been compromised by the pursuit of other U.S. interests such as protecting autocratic regimes from communist threats, obtaining access to military facilities, or garnering votes on key issues in the United Nations. With the demise of the Cold War, the United States need no longer ignore the abuse of human and political rights in its diplomatic and aid relationships. Emphasizing in our foreign policies the values cherished by Americans will bolster understanding and support for those policies at home.

Second, the mass of Africans, particularly the educated classes, aspire to the ideal of democracy. There was a time in the recent past when many Africans rejected democracy as an alien Western implant, a political system inappropriate to their needs. After thirty years of experimenting with a variety of authoritarian regimes, most Africans now regard them as failures, having deprived them both of their political rights and their hopes for a better economic future.

A third reason the United States should actively support the expansion and consolidation of democracy in Africa is that our words and our actions can make a major difference there. As the world's most powerful democracy, our voice has a resonance in Africa unlike that of any other power. We can also influence the policies of other Western governments vis-à-vis Africa by putting issues on the international agenda and by adopting policies that become a standard on which the publics of other nations judge their governments.

U.S. policy to promote democracy in Africa should have two elements: 1) Most important is the public and private expression of U.S. support for democratic change in the region; and 2) The United States should increase concessional resources to further democratic change.

While the United States has long favored the expansion of democracy throughout the world, other U.S. interests abroad have sometimes overridden or obscured U.S. support of democracy. As soon as possible, the new President should go on record in support of democracy in Africa and elsewhere. For maximum impact, his statement should include specific measures to promote democracy abroad as well as general statements supporting it. Senior U.S. officials and ambassadors in Africa must continue to go on record and be consistent in supporting democracy and opposing autocracy or backsliding by political leaders intent on staying in power at any cost. This includes public speeches, meetings with opposition leaders by U.S. ambassadors and prominent American visitors, private interventions with African leaders at critical moments to support political liberalization, and even, where appropriate, encouraging the departure of certain leaders to smooth a transition to a democratic regime. In the recent past—for example, in Zaïre—Washington has appeared reluctant to press President Mobutu publicly and vigorously to surrender power to an elected government. U.S. passivity there has not only weakened the credibility of U.S. support for democracy in Zaïre but also elsewhere in Africa.

Wherever possible, the United States must persuade or pressure other major powers with interests in particular countries to support similar policies both in private demarche and public statements. When the United States takes one position and the French or British governments take another, policy differences make it easier for the African leaders to ignore the views of Washington and Paris and London. Persuading the French government to support democratic changes may be a particular challenge since Paris (and particularly the Gaulist party) appears increasingly to equate democracy with destabilization in Africa—which it clearly need not be. It is also important that the major multilateral aid institutions be supportive of these policies since their resources help both to finance and to legitimize recipient governments.

In promoting democratic change in Africa, the United States should state what it believes to be the basic characteristics of a democratic political system, but it should not attempt to dictate the details of any particular system. The basic characteristics include freedom of speech and assembly (including the right to form political parties), an independent judiciary, and regular elections in which all adults can participate to choose candidates for legislative and (in presidential systems) executive positions. Whether a particular African political system is federal, confederal, consociational, or unitary, whether it is parliamentary or presidential, whether elected officials are chosen on the basis of a proportional or majority voting, whether the legislature is bicameral or unicameral, whether certain groups (e.g., ethnic or racial minorities) have entrenched rights, whether an upper house is elected or is made up of appointed traditional chiefs or others—all of these decisions should be taken by Africans themselves to fit their own social and political circumstances.

The United States has more than just its voice to use in support of democracy in Africa. It also has resources that can be deployed in furthering democratic change. Those resources can be used in two principal ways: 1) to finance activities that strengthen democratic forces in African countries; and 2) to reward progress toward democracy or punish governments that resist or reverse democratic reforms.

The United States already finances a variety of activities directly through the U.S. Agency for International Development and the U.S. Information Agency and indirectly through the National Endowment for Democracy, the National Democratic Institute for International Affairs, and the International Republican Institute. These activities are designed to strengthen the African media, support the development of nongovernmental organizations, strengthen local governments and community self-help activities, and train and provide election observers. The activities need to be linked to a broader strategy of promoting democracy in Africa and need to be pursued more consistently and vigorously by USAID officials. These types of activities are similar to those begun long ago with the U.S.-financed Asia Foundation and, after it was established in 1970s, by the Inter-American Foundation, an agency of the U.S. government.

The United States could do much more to strengthen democratic forces in Africa. It must continue to link the overall level of its aid on progress toward democracy and tie increases or decreases in aid to the degree of political reform. Countries that make good progress or already meet the minimum requirements for being considered democratic would receive larger aid flows; those resisting democratic change would be penalized by having their aid cut. U.S. law already requires that American aid be terminated when military regimes displace elected civilian governments.

This type of sanction would be most effective if other aid-giving governments and the multilateral development institutions followed similar policies.[17] Indeed, it may be meaningless without their support and cooperation since the United States is not a major source of aid in most of Sub-Saharan Africa. It must also be recognized that occasions may arise where such a sanction may not be warranted, for example, in the case of a weak civilian government unable to maintain domestic order or one that is wrecking the national economy. Some room for judgment should be left for foreign powers and international institutions to decide when to discontinue their aid because of political regression.

Indeed, many aspects of an effective policy of supporting democracy in Africa will require difficult political judgments. Holding elections is only one of many criteria considered in evaluating a country's progress in democratizing. Even elections are difficult to evaluate. For example, what is the United States to do when an incumbent president steals an election? Or, if there are widespread voting irregularities but the incumbent may have won enough honest votes to continue in office? In the several cases of this type that have already come up, the United States and other governments have tended to look the other way to preserve good relations with the government in question. This approach will quickly undermine a policy of supporting democratic change in Africa.

What is needed is a process that includes an objective determination of the progress toward democracy in African countries, combined with some flexibility for the administration to take into account other relevant factors in determining foreign aid levels and other policies. A possible model might be the creation of an international organization along the lines of Amnesty International to issue periodic reports on the governments' performance in extending and protecting the political rights of their citizens. Another model would be an annual report published by the Department of State or other U.S. government agency specifically on progress toward democracy abroad, similar to the reports State does on human rights throughout the world. These types of reports could provide the basis (but not the final judgment) for decisions on U.S. diplomatic postures and aid policies toward the Sub-Saharan African countries.

Two words of warning need to be sounded here. When the United States or other governments press Africans to implement political reforms, those governments assume a measure of responsibility for the consequences of their pressures. From both a practical and an ethical point of view, they should not encourage opposition movements only to turn away from them when governments attempt to repress them. To ensure that things do not go wrong, they need be consistent, to monitor the process of change, and to remain engaged where their interventions can smooth that process.

Second, aid-giving governments must be careful about how much financing they provide democratic forces in Sub-Saharan countries. Too much direct financing for African nongovernmental organizations, the media, or political parties could undermine their independence, reduce their incentives to finance themselves locally, and thus dull their responsiveness to the concerns of their clientele. A similar point may be made about rewarding governments for democratizing reforms. A dramatic increase in overall aid levels to particular governments can encourage the patronage-based politics of the past and undercut incentives for responsible governance.

. . . .

SUPPORTING DEVELOPMENT

■   DESPITE THE PROGRESS in social development of the past three decades, poverty, disease, illiteracy, economic decline, and despair rather than hope are still a way of life for many millions of Africans. Without assistance from abroad, even in the best circumstances and with the best intentions, it will be decades and perhaps more before the majority of Africans enjoy a minimally comfortable life.

The contribution of past assistance to African development has proven disappointing. To ensure that its aid promotes African development, the United States must review its past aid policies and identify a more effective set of assistance policies for the future.

The first task is to recognize mistakes. Perhaps the most important lesson is that aid provided for reasons other than supporting development should not be expected to promote development or rationalized as such. U.S. aid to Zaïre—long a major recipient of U.S. assistance—was not intended primarily to promote development but rather to bolster an inept and corrupt government that had been supportive of the U.S. policies. It was long feared that without U.S. support, Zaïre (large, strategically located, and rich in natural resources) might disintegrate or be taken over by a government friendly to Moscow. By strengthening Mobutu's regime, the United States may have inadvertently prolonged the economic disaster Mobutu brought to his people.

It is now widely recognized that aid for development must be tailored to the conditions of the recipient country if they are to be effective in promoting development. Past failures of aid in Africa—and there have been many—have often resulted from the use of aid to implement policies ill-suited to local conditions. Aid donors have often been in too quick to commit their resources, too mesmerized by grand theories for promoting worldwide development, too constrained by development policies derived from experience at home or elsewhere in the world, too little informed about Africa, and too unwilling to spend enough time consulting Africans about what they wanted and needed. The great Integrated Rural Development debacle during the 1970s and early 1980s was one such casualty. Western donors financed many expensive rural development projects that were inappropriate to African conditions, had little impact on the region's development, and have now all but vanished.

A third lesson from the past, too seldom recognized, is that development cannot be bought with foreign aid alone. Governments have to want development, and their peoples must have a hand in shaping it. Low-income African countries are among the most aided in the world, with annual aid flows often equal to 100 percent of the level of national investment and 15 percent of gross domestic product. But where policies or the behavior of political leaders do not support growth, investment—

whether financed by external assistance, domestic savings, or foreign investors—has in the past and will in the future prove unproductive.

Past experience has shown us what not to do with aid in Africa, and it has also provided some guidelines for the future.

First, the United States should continue to press for needed economic reforms in Africa. African governments cannot go on indefinitely spending more than they earn. Neither can African economies grow if government policies and the behavior of public officials is such as to discourage productive investment and growth. At the same time, the United States should recognize that some reforms are more important than others to economic recovery and future growth, and that African governments, for both administrative and political reasons, cannot implement large numbers of reforms in short periods of time. Priorities and pacing are important, and the advice of Africans on what reforms are most needed and politically feasible is critical and should be sought. However, the United States should not take a leading role in promoting economic reforms in Africa in the future. It has neither the capacity nor the resources to do so. That role should remain with the World Bank and IMF.

Second, the United States can make an important contribution in the social sector, largely neglected during the early 1980s, as was evidenced by the precipitous decline in the extent and quality of social services and infrastructure. In the process of reform public investments in human resource development and infrastructure must be maintained if future growth is to occur and poverty is to be reduced. Significant and sustained improvements in the standard of living of the mass of Africans will come only with economic growth. For the poor to enjoy the benefits of that growth, men and women must be healthy, educated, and able to participate in the national economy. Donors have returned to financing projects in the social sectors, and this policy needs to be continued and even strengthened.

A third area where the United States has been widely regarded as having a particular expertise is institutional development. It should once more turn its attention to ways of strengthening institutions in Africa, especially public institutions. Strong institutions will remain a key to economic progress.

PUTTING IT ALL TOGETHER

■   THE POLICIES RECOMMENDED in the previous three sections
may all make sense individually but melding them into a coherent policy
toward Sub-Saharan Africa will not be easy. Though interconnected, the
three major problems identified in this essay and the policies recommended to meet them contain potential contradictions. Successful political
reform may slow economic reform. Rewarding political reform with
increased foreign aid can ease pressures for economic reform. Rapid economic reform or poorly managed political reform can provoke political
unrest and undermine the new democracies. How can U.S. policies
intended to advance one goal be shaped to avoid undermining the others?
Clearly, prioritization and integration are needed to ensure consistency.

The top priority should be maintaining peace and security in
African countries. Without peace, there will be neither development nor
democracy. The United States should take the initiative immediately to
promote agreement on guidelines and mechanisms to deal with conflicts
in Africa, perhaps by appointing an ambassador-at-large with responsibility for pursuing this issue. The United States should also set aside part
of its economic and military assistance to support African governments
that are attempting to resolve internal conflicts. Where African governments persist in policies that generate such conflicts, the United States
should express its displeasure by reducing its aid and perhaps its diplomatic presence in those countries. In both instances, the United States
should coordinate wherever possible with other governments, both European and African.

Foreign aid should be provided to promote both democracy and
development without undermining either one of them. This can be accom-
plished in the following fashion. African governments observing basic
human rights and making progress on extending political rights or consolidating democratic reforms would receive a "core" aid program to finance
projects in human resource development and infrastructure, as well as
for strengthening democratic forces. The greater the progress toward
democratization, the larger this core program would be. Where, in the
judgment of independent observers and the U.S. government, progress

on political reform was inadequate or reversed (for example, holding sham elections), the core aid program would be scaled back or suspended. Humanitarian relief would continue to be provided directly to the needy regardless of the political system.

Where governments make good progress on both political and economic reforms, additional aid would be provided—beyond the core—to finance projects or imports tied to human resource development.

In these cases, debt relief should also be offered. The United States could, for example, cancel bilateral debt equivalent to the amount due in debt servicing during an agreed period. This would reduce the amount of foreign exchange governments would have to give up to pay their debts, thus increasing the amount they had for imports. It would also reduce the overall stock of debt which, for many African countries is very large relative to the size of their economies and can diminish future growth prospects. In contrast to current debt-rescheduling arrangements, the approach would not involve canceling a country's total debt owed the United States, but it would provide incentives for continued good performance on political and economic reforms.[18] After a period of good performance in both areas, any arrears on past debts could be canceled or reduced by an increasing proportion for each year of good behavior.

Linking the amount of aid to progress on both political and economic reforms would provide the basis for a coherent U.S. policy toward Africa. It would reflect U.S. values and support the aspirations of the vast majority of Africans for peace, political freedom, and better lives for themselves and their children. We should do no less.

Notes

[1] This essay is concerned only with the countries of Africa south of the Sahara. Statistical materials and discussion, unless otherwise noted, do not include Morocco, Algeria, Tunisia, Libya, or Egypt. For convenience, "Africa" will be used to refer to Sub-Saharan Africa.

[2] One of the best descriptions of the systems of "personal rule" that appeared so widely in Africa over the past thirty years is Robert H. Jackson and Carl G. Rosberg, in *Personal Rule in Black Africa: Prince, Autocrat, Prophet, Tyrant* (Berkeley: University of California Press, 1982).

[3] Overvalued exchange rates encourage imports of food from abroad and discourage exports.

[4] Michael Clough, *Free at Last: US Policy Toward Africa and the End of the Cold War* (New York: Council on Foreign Relations, 1992), p. 12.

[5] This statement is based on interviews with former Soviet officials responsible for Africa.

[6] Development Assistance Committee, *Development Co-Operation 1992* (Paris: OECD Publications, 1992), p. A-5.

[7] International Monetary Fund, *Direction of Trade Statistics Yearbook* (Washington, DC: IMF, 1965 and 1992).

[8] Eritrea is not an ethnically or religiously homogenous territory. Its people share a sense of distinctiveness from the rest of Ethiopia based on their historical experience as part of the Italian colonial empire. After the World War II, they demanded independence from Ethiopia. The West, acceding to Emperor Selassie's desires, agreed that Eritrea would be incorporated into Ethiopia as an autonomous province and did not object later when its autonomy was extinguished.

[9] Joan Nelson with Stephanie J. Eglinton, *Encouraging Democracy: What Role for Conditioned Aid?* (Washington, DC: ODC, 1992).

[10] This group includes the Côte d'Ivoire, Ghana, Guinea-Bissau, Kenya, Madagascar, Malawi, Mauritania, Mauritius, Nigeria, Senegal, Tanzania, Togo, and Zambia. These are countries that received two or more structural adjustment loans by June 1990 and the first loan before June 1986. This is, however, a dubious basis for grouping these countries together. Receiving adjustment loans does not mean that the loan conditions were implemented or maintained. For example, the Côte d'Ivoire, Senegal, Togo, Kenya, and Zambia have had limited success in implementing economic reforms. Kenya has resisted a number of reform measures urged on it by the international community. Zambia has not implemented a sustained program of reforms. The weakness of the criteria for this grouping raises questions about the analyses of the economic impact of adjustment. See World Bank, Country Economics Department, *Adjustment Lending and Mobilization of Private and Public Resources for Growth*, Policy and Research Series 22 (Washington, DC: World Bank, 1992).

[11] The World Bank suggests that to achieve a target rate of 4 percent annual growth, Africans need to invest 25 percent and save 18 percent of their GDP each year. Net foreign transfers

from abroad—primarily foreign aid—is assumed to make up the rest. See World Bank, *Sub-Saharan Africa: From Crisis to Sustainable Growth* (Washington, DC: World Bank, 1989), p. 13.

[12] Ibid., Table A2.4, p. 84.

[13] Nicolas Van de Walle, "The Decline of the Franc Zone: Monetary Policies in Francophone Africa," *African Affairs* (1991), p. 90; and Olivier Vallée, *La Prix de l'Argent CFA: Heures et Malheurs de la Zone Franc,* (Paris: Karthala, 1989).

[14] Nicolas Van de Walle, op. cit., p. 403.

[15] World Bank, *Sub-Saharan Africa*, op. cit.

[16] The Asian tigers include Singapore, Hong Kong, Taiwan, and South Korea.

[17] The articles of agreement of multilateral financial institutions like the World Bank, typically prohibit their intervention in member states' political systems or lending decisions based on political considerations. However, the World Bank has demonstrated how flexible this prohibition is in reducing its lending to Kenya and Malawi pending political reforms in those countries and in its pressures on those governments to implement such reforms. The Bank's rationale for linking lending to political reforms has been that because poor governance arising from authoritarian political systems impedes development, it is a legitimate development concern to the Bank. This view is a logical extension of the Bank's development mission and the recognition that the quality of governance is important. But it remains controversial both within the Bank and among its borrowers in Africa.

[18] This approach differs from the Toronto Menu Approach or the proposed Trinidad Terms in that it cancels *all* bilateral debt due over the course of a year. But that does *not* cancel debt due in future years. For more details on all these proposals, see Carol Lancaster, *African Economic Reform: The External Dimension* (Washington, DC: Institute for International Economics, 1991).

Acknowledgments

I wish to thank those who were kind enough to read and comment on this essay: David Gordon, Alison Rosenberg, Catherine Gwin, Christine Contee, and John Sewell. And thanks go to my research assistant, Melissa Brown, for help on details and fact checking. The final product is, of course, my responsibility.

About the Author

CAROL LANCASTER, assistant professor at Georgetown University, is currently the Davidson Sommers Fellow at ODC. She has written many articles and books on African political economy and politics, economic development, and U.S. policies toward Africa. She has also worked for the Office of Management and Budget, Congress, and the Department of State, where she was a Deputy Assistant Secretary of State for Africa.

About the ODC

ODC fosters an understanding of how development relates to a much changed U.S. domestic and international policy agenda and helps shape the new course of global development cooperation.

ODC's programs focus on three main issues: the challenge of political and economic transitions and the reform of development assistance programs; the development dimensions of international global problems; and the implications of development for U.S. economic security.

In pursuing these themes, ODC functions as:

■ *A center for policy analysis.* Bridging the worlds of ideas and actions, ODC translates the best academic research and analysis on selected issues of policy importance into information and recommendations for policymakers in the public and private sectors.

■ *A forum for the exchange of ideas.* ODC's conferences, seminars, workshops, briefings bring together legislators, business executives, scholars, and representatives of international financial institutions and nongovernmental groups.

■ *A resource for public education.* Through its publications, meetings, testimony, lectures, and formal and informal networking, ODC makes timely, objective, nonpartisan information available to an audience that includes but reaches far beyond the Washington policymaking community.

ODC is a private, nonprofit organization funded by foundations, corporations, governments, and private individuals.

Stephen J. Friedman is the Chairman of the Overseas Development Council, and John W. Sewell is the Council's President.

Board of Directors

Overseas Development Council

SPECIAL PUBLICATIONS SUBSCRIPTION OFFER

Policy Essays • Policy Focus

As a subscriber to the ODC's 1993 publication series, you will have access to an invaluable source of independent analyses of U.S.-Third World issues—economic, political, and social—at a savings of at least 10% off the regular price.

Brief and easy-to-read, each **Policy Focus** briefing paper provides background information and analysis on a current topic on the policy agenda. In 1993, 6–8 papers will cover the Bretton Woods institutions and the former Soviet Union, the Global Environment Facility, the Generalized System of Preferences, and the implications of the North American Free Trade Area, among other topics.

Policy Essays explore critical issues on the U.S.-Third World agenda in 80-120 succinct pages, offering concrete recommendations for action. The two final essays in the "conditionality" series, *Pro-Poor Aid Conditionality* and *Global Goals, Contentious Means: Issues of Multiple Aid Conditionality*, will explore the potential utility of applying conditionality for the goal of poverty reduction and the implications of multiple aid conditionality—linking political, environmental, military, and pro-poor reforms to foreign aid.

Global Governance and Aid After the Earth Summit will assess the international institutional capabilities that now exist for carrying through on the UNCED commitments of sustainable development.

United States and Africa: Into the 21st Century examines the pressing regional challenges of ending civil conflict, expanding and consolidating democracy, and achieving economic recovery and sustainable growth. It also assesses options for future U.S. policy.

SUBSCRIPTION OPTIONS

Special Publications Subscription Offer* (all Policy Essays (5–6) and Policy Focus briefing papers (6–8) issued in 1993)	$65.00
1993 Policy Essay Subscription*	$50.00
Policy Focus Subscription*	$20.00

* Subscribers will receive all 1993 publications issued to date upon receipt of payment; other publications in subscription will be sent upon release. Book-rate postage is included in price.

All orders require prepayment. Visa and Mastercard orders accepted by phone or mail. Please send check or money order to:

O | D | C

Publication Orders
Overseas Development Council
1875 Connecticut Avenue, NW
Suite 1012
Washington, DC 20009
(202) 234-8701